Let's Play Dress Up
I WANT TO BE A FAIRY

Rebekah Joy Shirley
Photography by Chris Fairclough

WINDMILL
BOOKS

New York

Published in 2012 by Windmill Books, An Imprint of Rosen Publishing
29 East 21st Street, New York, NY 10010

Series concept: Discovery Books Ltd, 2 College Street, Ludlow, Shropshire SY8 1AN
www.discoverybooks.net

Managing editor: Laura Durman
Editor: Rebecca Hunter
Designer: Blink Media
Photography: Chris Fairclough

Library of Congress Cataloging-in-Publication Data

Shirley, Rebekah Joy.
  I Want to Be a Fairy / By Rebekah Joy Shirley. — First edition.
     pages cm — (Let's Play Dress Up)
  Includes bibliographical references and index.
  ISBN 978-1-61533-358-5 (library binding : alk. paper) — ISBN 978-1-61533-396-7 (pbk. : alk. paper) — ISBN
978-1-61533-479-7 (6-pack : alk. paper)
  1. Handicraft--Juvenile literature. 2. Children's costumes—Juvenile literature. 3. Fairies—Juvenile literature. I.
Title.
  TT171.S545 2012
  646.4'78—dc22
                              2010047725

The author and photographer would like to acknowledge the following for their help in preparing this book:
the staff and pupils of Chad Vale Primary School, Jack Coady, Iqrah Choudhury, Ayla-Belma Hadzovic,
Sunny Marko-Bennett, Abbie Sangha.

Printed in China

CPSIA Compliance Information: Batch #AS2011WM: For Further Information contact Windmill Books, New York, New York at 1-866-478-0556
SL001742US

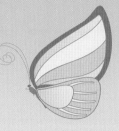

CONTENTS

Some of the projects in this book require the use of needles, pins, and safety pins.
We would advise that young children are supervised by a responsible adult.

A FAIRYTALE DRESS

Woodland fairies live in a secret world of their own. They wear clothes made from leaves and flowers.

Make a forest fairy outfit using:

- An undershirt or T-shirt
- An unused green trash bag
- Colored plastic bags (preferably green, yellow, and orange)
- 3-ft length of green ribbon
- Scotch tape
- A pair of scissors
- A needle and thread
- A ruler

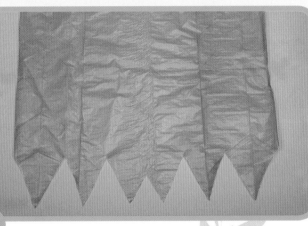

1 Cut the trash bag to the length that you want your skirt to be. Cut triangles out of the bottom edge.

2 Ask an adult to help you cut two slits in the middle at the top of the bag. The slits should be about 2 in. apart and 1 in. from the top of the bag. Pull the ends of the ribbon through the slits that you have made. The ribbon ends should be inside the bag.

3 Fold the top edge of the bag over so that the ribbon is hidden and the ends are now outside the bag. Stick tape along the edge to hold in it place.

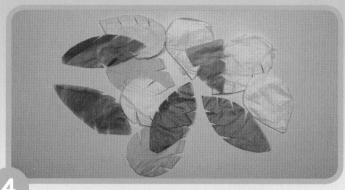

4 Cut leaf shapes out of different colored plastic bags.

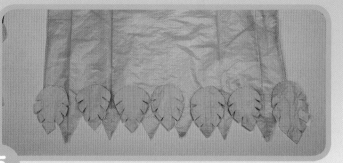

5 Using Scotch tape, fix a row of leaf shapes at the bottom of the trash bag.

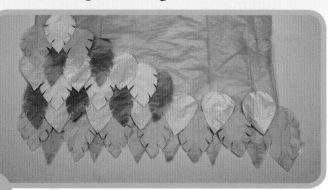

6 Stick another row of leaves above the first row, **overlapping** it slightly. Continue adding rows until the bag is covered.

7 Sew the leaf shapes to your T-shirt or undershirt. Sew two stitches at the top of each leaf.

Carefully put on your fairy top. Then tie the ribbon around your waist to wear your skirt. You're ready to play in the forest!

FLUTTERING WINGS

Fairies fly using their beautiful, sparkly wings. Fairy wings are very **fragile** and must be handled with care.

To make your own wings you will need:

- Four metal coat hangers
- A pair of colored pantyhose
- Scotch tape
- 15 tinsel pipe cleaners
- Styrofoam balls
- Craft glue and a paintbrush
- 20 ft. of sequin ribbon
- A pair of scissors
- 40-in. length of elastic

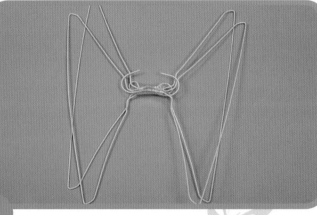

1 Take two coat hangers and join them at the twisted part by the hooks. Use Scotch tape to secure. Then attach the other two coat hangers on top of them in the same way.

2 Cut the top off the pair of pantyhose. Cut each leg in half.

3 Stretch these four pieces over the wire wing-shapes and tie at the back. Ask an adult to straighten the hooks.

4 Glue **Styrofoam** balls to the end of each straightened hook and wrap tinsel pipe cleaners around them.

5 Glue sequin ribbon around the edges of the wings and to cover the joined area in the middle.

Put your arms through the elastic loops and flutter away with your fairy friends!

6 Glue tinsel pipe cleaners onto the wings in curly patterns and shapes.

7 Cut two 20-in. lengths of elastic. Tie them to the middle of the wings to make two loops.

FAIRY FEET

Fairies wear beautiful, **dainty** shoes on their feet so that they can skip silently through the forest.

Make your own fairy slippers using:
Fun foam
A hole punch
Ten lengths of ribbon, each about 20 in. long, in three or four different colors
A pair of scissors
A ruler

1 Draw around a pair of your shoes on a piece of fun foam. Then cut the shapes out.

TIP:
If the foam is too thick to use a hole punch, ask an adult to make the holes in the foam for you.

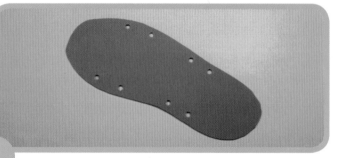

3 Punch four holes toward the back of each shoe as shown above.

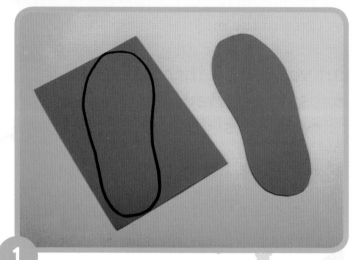

2 Punch four holes at the front of each shoe as shown in the picture. The holes should be about an inch apart and half an inch from the edge.

4 Thread three of the ribbons through the front holes. Thread them in a crisscross pattern.

5 Bring the ends of the ribbons up through the front two holes at the back of each shoe. Tie a knot at each end of the ribbons.

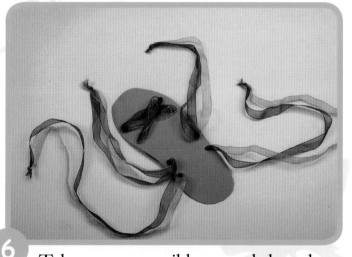

6 Take two more ribbons and thread them through the two holes at the very back of each shoe. Then tie a knot at the ends.

Tie the ribbons in a crisscross way finishing with a bow at the back of your leg. Now you are ready to skip through the forest in your fantastic fairy footwear.

FLOWERS FOR A FAIRY

Fairies love to gather flowers from the forests and meadows. Make this bunch of flowers and little ladybug to impress your fairy friends.

To make your own flowers you will need:
Colored tissue paper
Green pipe cleaners
A pair of scissors
Red and black felt
Two plastic eyes
Craft glue and a paintbrush
A ruler

1 Cut the tissue paper into rectangles about 2 in. by 6 in.

TIP:
For smaller flowers make smaller rectangles.

2 Fold each piece of tissue paper backward and forward down the length of the paper until the whole rectangle is folded up. Then tie one end of a pipe cleaner around the middle.

3 Trim the ends of the tissue paper strip. You could cut the end into a point or a rounded shape.

4 Gently spread out the paper folds on both sides to make a flower shape. Repeat to make a whole **bouquet**.

Glue the ladybug onto a flower. Carry your beautiful flowers with you wherever you go. You could also use them to decorate your hair, clothing, and shoes.

5 Cut out a circle of red felt about 1 ½ in. in diameter. Also cut out an oval of black felt and four small circles.

6 Glue them all to the red circle.

7 Glue two plastic eyes to the ladybug.

A "MAKE-A-WISH" WAND

Fairies carry a magic wand with them wherever they go. They use the wand to **grant** wishes.

Make your own wand using:
- A ruler
- A pen or pencil
- Cardboard
- Metallic foiled paper
- Craft glue and a paintbrush
- Sequins
- Craft gems
- 1-ft. length of $\frac{1}{2}$ in. dowel
- 3-ft. length of ribbon
- Scotch tape
- A pair of scissors

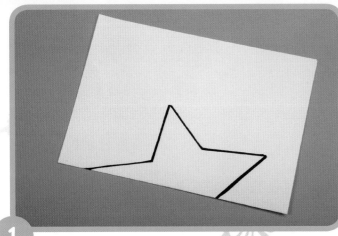

1 Fold a piece of cardboard in half. Use a ruler to draw half a star onto the cardboard along the fold.

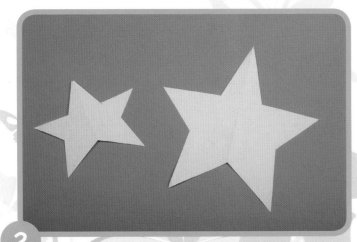

2 Cut out the shape and unfold the star. Then draw a smaller star in the same way.

3 Draw around the star shapes on metallic foiled paper. Cut the shapes out.

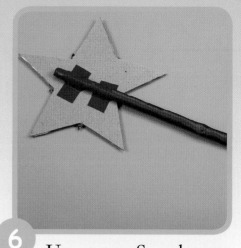

4 Glue the metallic paper onto the cardboard stars and glue the stars together. Decorate with craft gems and sequins.

5 Glue one end of the ribbon to the bottom of the dowel. Wrap the ribbon around the dowel and tape it at the end.

6 Use strong Scotch tape to attach the dowel to the back of the star.

Now wave your wand and make someone's dream come true. Whose wish will you grant first?

A HEAVENLY HEADBAND

Woodland fairies wear beautiful headbands made of forest **vines**, leaves, and flowers.

1 Make a crown as the base of your headband by wrapping ten pipe cleaners around each other to form a circle. The circle needs to fit comfortably on your head.

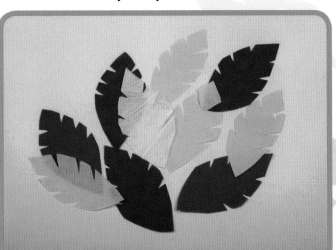

2 Cut leaf shapes out of colored paper or plastic.

3 Make some small paper flowers in the same way as you did on page 10.

14

4 Repeat to make two wing shapes on the other side. Then pull another pipe cleaner out on each side and leave them loose.

5 Continue wrapping the pipe cleaner from step 2 around the body until it is about 4 in. long. Cut off the end.

Use the two loose pipe cleaners to attach the butterfly to your arm. What a beautiful fairy friend!

6 Cut out four wing shapes from metallic cardboard. Decorate them with glitter glue and gems.

7 Use Scotch tape to attach the cardboard wings to the pipe cleaner loops.

FAIRY DUST

Fairies use **enchanting** sparkles and dust to spread magic. They carry the fairy dust around in a special pouch.

Make your own fairy dust pouch using:
- An old sock
- Ribbon
- A wool needle
- A pair of scissors
- Sequins
- A ruler

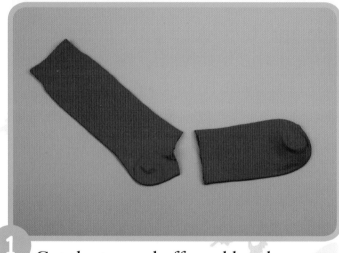

1 Cut the toe end off an old sock so you are left with a pouch about 6 in. long.

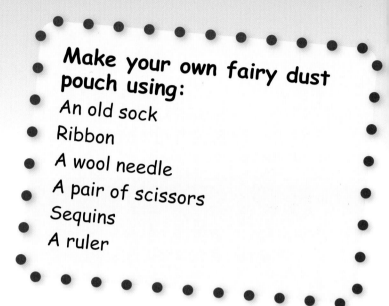

2 Thread the ribbon onto a large wool needle. Weave it in and out of the top edge of sock. You can use the two loose ends later to close the pouch.

3 Cut three 20-in. lengths of ribbon. Plait the ribbons together. Then repeat with another three 20-in. lengths of ribbon.

4 Tie one of the plaits through a ribbon loop on the left-hand side of the pouch. Tie the other plait through a loop on the right-hand side.

5 Fill the pouch with sequins.

Tie the plaited ribbons around your waist. Now you can sprinkle magical fairy dust whenever it is needed!

A FAIRY'S BEST FRIEND

Some of the fairies' best friends are the elves that live in the forest. Elves are very **mischievous** and love to play games and have fun.

1 Cut triangles out of the bottom of the T-shirt. Cut triangles along the sleeve edges, too.

TIP: You could follow the instructions for the fairy dress to cover your elf T-shirt in leaves if you like.

2 Measure around your waist with a tape measure. Cut a strip of brown felt that is 2 in. wide and 8 in. longer than your waist measurement.

3 Cut out a circle of brown felt about 20 in. across. Cut triangles around the edge.

4 Fold the circle in half and cut a small semicircle out of the middle through both layers.

5 Cut a quarter circle with a **radius** of about 12 in., out of green felt. Glue the edges together to make a cone shaped hat.

TIP:
If you don't have a jingle bell, you could glue a pompom to the top of the hat instead.

6 Glue or sew a jingle bell to the top of the hat.

Become an elf by putting on the T-shirt, collar, and belt. Then pop your hat on your head. Pull it down on one side to give your outfit an impish look!

23

GLOSSARY

antennae (an-TEH-nee) the long, thin "feelers" on an insect's head
bouquet (boo-KAY) a bunch of flowers
creature (KREE-chur) an animal
dainty (DAYN-tee) delicate and pretty
enchanting (en-CHANT-ing) magical
fragile (FRA-jul) delicate and easily broken
grant (GRANT) to give something as a favor
mischievous (MIS-chuh-vis) playful and naughty
overlap (oh-ver-LAP) to put part of one thing on top of another
radius (RAY-dee-us) the measurement between the center of a circle and its edge
Styrofoam (STY-ruh-fohm) a white, foamlike material
vine (VYN) a plant that creeps and twists its way through other plants

FURTHER INFORMATION

Clibbon, Meg and Clibbon, Lucy. *The Fairyspotter's Guide.* Midwest City, OK: Zero to Ten, 2007.

Kane, Barry and Kane, Tracy. *Fairy Houses and Beyond!* Lee, NH: Light-Beams Publishing, 2008.

Marriott, Susannah. *A Field Guide to Fairies.* Hauppauge, NY: Barron's Educational Series, 2009.

WEB SITES

For Web resources related to the subject of this book, go to:
www.windmillbooks.com/weblinks and select this book's title.

INDEX